RTI Success Stories in India

A look to Funny & Serious RTI Success Stories in India

<u>By Asha Kanta Sharma</u>

<u>Guwahati, Assam, India</u>

<u>1st January 2020</u>

ABSTRACT

The book lists out several the funny in addition to serious success testimonies using the energy of the Right to Information (RTI) Act in India. Corruption do have very harmful effects on financial and political development. Corruption together of the oldest phenomenon in human society exist in each country times. Corruption are regularly defined in a few ways like preferred sickness of body politics, public exploitation and abuse of position for personal gain. The causes of corruption also are many in number. For instance, cultural element, psychological element and system related factors may additionally reason corruption in each society. There are a few factors like monopoly energy, discretionary electricity and weak responsibility of public officials can also give opportunities for corrupt acts. Corruption may also decrease the performance of public spending, lower the budget revenues, raise the deficit, restrict Foreign Direct Investment, reduce the effectiveness the usage of aid, deplete political legitimacy and hinders the democratic development. The anticorruption marketing campaign need to mainly don't forget the reforms of government officials, judiciary machine, tax, and custom departments.

Let's use the power of RTI and make the Govt Accountable.

TABLE OF CONTENTS

Part – 1: Serious RTI Success Stories in India

Part – 2: Funny RTI Stories in India

Part – 1:

Serious RTI Success Stories in India

The Right-to-Information Act has emerged as a powerful tool for India's civil society to make transparency and preserve those in strength accountable. The law, which allows Indian citizens to are looking for data from most government bodies, was first carried out in October 2005.

Adarsh Housing Society, Commonwealth Games, and 2G are just a few of the scams and scandals that spring to thoughts whilst musing approximately the impact of the Right to Information Act, over the last several 12 months. And even as the RTI, which came into force on October 12, 2005, has uncovered the rot and corruption of the country's establishments and leaders, it has also played a large role in improving the daily lives of humans by making government available and accountable.

The sweep of questions and concerns protected in tens of hundreds of thousands of RTI packages is impossible to catalogue, however whether or not it is looking for entitlements, exposing hoarding at nearby ration shops, or getting a village avenue constructed, these queries and proceedings are all guided by the principle of standing up and being counted.

The underneath is serious successful RTI cases:

• Adarsh Society Scam:

The packages filed via RTI activists like Yogacharya Anandji and Simpreet Singh in 2008 had been instrumental in bringing to light links among politicians and army officers, amongst others. The 31-storey building, which had permission for 6 floors simplest, turned into originally supposed to house war widows and veterans. Instead, the residences went to several politicians, bureaucrats, and their relatives. The scandal has already led to the resignation of Ashok Chavan, the former leader minister of Maharashtra. Other state officials are also under the scanner.

- Public Distribution Scam in Assam:

In 2007, contributors of an anti-corruption non-governmental business enterprise based totally in Assam, the Krishak Mukti Sangram Samiti, filed an RTI request that found out irregularities within the distribution of food supposed for humans beneath the poverty line. The allegations of corruption have been probed and numerous authorities' officials arrested.

- Appropriation of Relief Funds:

Information obtained through an RTI application by using an NGO based totally in Punjab, in 2008 found out that bureaucrats heading local branches of the Indian Red Cross Society used cash supposed for victims of the Kargil warfare and natural disasters to shop for cars, air-conditioners and pay for inn bills – among other things. Local courts charged the officials found responsible with fraud and the funds were transferred to the Prime Minister's Relief Fund.

- IIM's Admission Criteria:

Vaishnavi Kasturi a visually-impaired scholar, in 2007 became denied a seat in the Indian Institute of Management in Bangalore, one of the country's premier control institutes – despite her impressive rating at the doorway examination. Ms. Kasturi wanted to understand why and wondered whether it was because of her physical disability. She filed an RTI utility to request the institute to disclose their selection process. Although she failed to benefit admission to the institute, her RTI utility intended that IIM had to make its admission standards public. It emerged that the doorway exam, the Common Admission Test, sincerely mattered little compared to Class 10 and 12 results.

- Absconding Teacher:

Soon after the Act got here into force, parents in Panchampur village within the district of Banda, Uttar Pradesh, used it to music their nearby school instructor, who hardly ever made an appearance in the classroom.

After learning from RTI activists that they may want to are seeking attendance and leave statistics of the authorities school instructor, 15 villagers filed an application asking about his whereabouts, and also puzzled the duty of the Primary Education Department in such a situation.

Immediate action become taken: a new faculty trainer was appointed to the village faculty, and an enquiry turned into ordered in opposition to the absconder.

- Chandigarh–Smoke Free City:

In 2007, Chandigarh became the first smoke unfastened metropolis in India, which meant banning smoke in indoor spaces as well as prohibiting it in outside public places likes parks and markets.

But Hemant Ghosh didn't count on his RTI packages to steer to one of these landmark selections, which would impact different cities to enforce smoke-free laws in the years to come. His paintings are widely seemed like the cause for the campaign to create focus about the hazards of smoking, concerning public provider messages on tv and cinemas, which has grown over the years.

Soon after the Act came into force, Ghosh flooded the governments of Punjab and Haryana with over three hundred queries on how The Cigarettes and Other Tobacco Products Act (COTPA), which sets out provisions to deal with smoking in public places, became being implemented in their shared capital.

According to the 2003 law, his application asked whether the No Smoking Area Smoking right here is an offence caution was displayed in workplaces and premises below authorities' control."

In 2007, 1,800 "caution boards" regarded in all government departments, police stations, hospitals and schools.

Ghosh, who heads a Chandigarh-based NGO referred to as Burning Brain Society, stated that he changed into handiest attempting to maintain the government accountable. "What has been maximum pleasurable is to peer this replicated across the country," he stated.

Almost ten years on, however, any other RTI application filed by means of Gaurav Bansal, a 21-year-vintage resident of Chandigarh, discovered that due to his simple RTI, seventy eight people had been fined for smoking in public in 2013, which covered 61 people in only the one vicinity of region 19.

"Despite the claims of the management to make the town a smoke-free one, most effective 78 persons have been challenged (fined) in a whole year," he stated.

- The Seven Ponds:

In 2010, K.S. Sagaria smelt a rat whilst the paperwork showed that seven ponds have been built for under poverty lines families in Kushmal village of Orissa, but no one inside the village may want to spot them.

So, he filed an RTI application which discovered that the ponds were in no way dug, the "labourers" who worked to "construct" the ponds included dead human beings.

Following complaints, the management suspended the officers involved inside the subterfuge, and the assignment turned into renewed, but this time, the villagers vowed to hold a test on its progress.

- Scholarships for Students:

While several of his classmates and their dad and mom have been fretting when they didn't receive their scholarships for the instructional year of 2011-2012, 9-12 months-old Manoj, a scholar on the government primary school in Vailpoor, Nizamabad district of Telangana, filed an application.

In his application directed on the Labour Welfare Department, the class four scholar requested why the money had no longer reached the college students, and by using when they ought to assume their scholarships.

Manoj's RTI application secured scholarships for 10 college students, who're the kids of beedi workers.

- School Uniforms:

When students of Gulrahai Primary School in Allahabad did not acquire their school uniforms in December 2006, nine parents filed an RTI Application questioning the management approximately about the missing uniforms, which led to school attire being introduced inside the first week of January, 2007.

Parents of a central authority faculty in Chitrakoot, Uttar Pradesh, also procured school uniforms through filing an RTI application.

- Unjustifiable regulations imposed by means of CBSE on the examinees:

A need to- read records which can be useful to a large wide variety of our fellow residents. A landmark decision with respect to unjustifiable restrictions imposed with the aid of Central Board of Secondary Education (CBSE), Patna on the examinees delivered by using Central Information Commissioner (CIC) Prof. M. Sridhar Acharyulu (Madabhushi Sridhar). This is one of the quality decisions delivered ever through CIC which may be useful to a huge cross section of society.

The appellant, father of a pupil has sought copies of the answer sheets of his son for the subjects Maths and Science of twelfth Class exam seemed in 2013 and the related matters. The statistics sought changed into denied by using CPIO on the subsequent grounds:

1. The request for the deliver of evaluated answer sheets turned into made, no longer by way of the candidate, who regarded within the examination, but with the aid of his father, as the guidelines framed by the CBSE vide its Notification dated 17.06.2013 mandates the candidate ought to make application.

2. The last date for the receipt of requests via on-line for the delivery of evaluated solution sheets was 03.07.2013, and the RTI request, made through the candidate's father turned into 12.8.2013.

3. Requests/applications for supply of solution sheets ought to be made only thru online within 10 days from the date of statement of the result. After downloading the hardcopy of the printout of the request/confirmation page, from the website, the candidate ought to get the equal reached to the CBSE office, before the specified date, alongside the fee and different prescribed enclosures.

5. Among the files to be enclosed together with the application, there's an assignment from the candidate, written in his personal handwriting and beneath his personal signature and no longer with the aid of every person else on his behalf. The signature ought to correspond to that present on the Admit Card of the candidate. The candidate cannot question the assessment executed by the examiner. The candidate

can simply point out the errors in the totaling of marks, or the answers which were no longer evaluated by the examiner. These errors must be communicated by using the candidate in writing to the CBSE inside 10 days from the date of receipt of the evaluated answer sheets. There is not any provision within the CBSE Rules, for the revaluation of the answer sheets again.

6. The candidate must also adopt that the copies of his solution sheets shall no longer take delivery of to any group or faculty for display, business purpose or to print media.

The Commission taken into consideration that the respondent authority has created several unreasonable conditions to either limit or put off and deny the proper to records of the scholar who appeared for the exam conducted via CBSE in 2013. The reasonability and legality or validity or in any other case of the contentions of the CBSE are given below:

1. The CBSE has no authority to impose such limit at the rights of minor and his mother or father. The natural mother or father (father) has a felony responsibility and authority to steady the rights and benefits of the minor boy. In that capability he has every right to seeking for proper to records of his son be applied and any injustice taking place to his son in assessment of his answer scripts which might affect his career forever. The CBSE did now not provide an explanation for in reasonable phrases why it has denied the natural mum or dad from exercise his felony responsibility to stable the legal pursuits of his son inclusive of his right to facts. Hence the reason mentioned to deny the 'father' is unreasonable and illegal and additionally in violation of rights of the minor boy. The CBSE has no authority to impose such restriction at the rights of juvenile and his guardian. Hence the Commission holds that the appellant who is the father of the candidate is entitled for the copies of the solution sheets of his son, which shall be supplied to him.

2. Application turned into submitted past last date prescribed by means of the CBSE. The appellant has exercised his proper to information under RTI Act, 2005 in line with which the public authority ought to give records held by way of it. The CBSE has not denied the fact of holding the answer scripts of the son of appellant as at the date of RTI application. Once the RTI has been filed, it has no authority to destroy the answer scripts since the demand below statute is pending. Hence the competition that appellant approached past the remaining date does no longer maintain good underneath RTI Act.

3. The candidate must sign assignment papers relinquishing his right to re-evaluation has been imposed unreasonably. If a student has a legally recognized right to re-assessment, why should he relinquish it really because he wanted to work out every other legal right to records through seeking to have replica of the answer script? The reputation and making sure of proper to information are geared toward making the public authority 'accountable'. But by using imposing this condition the CBSE isn't simplest

proscribing that proper to facts, but also insulating itself from being accountable. This condition that scholar ought to log off his rights by means of a task is a severe obstruction to right to facts of teenybopper boy and his dad or mum.

4. Condition to relinquish proper to percentage answer script with others, media to query the incorrect evaluation etc. Another unreasonable situation imposed via CBSE is that candidate shall now not show answer script after obtaining it under RTI Act. He ought to not percentage with print media also. These are unconstitutional regulations on the proper to freedom of speech and expression guaranteed through Article 19(1)(a) of Indian Constitution.

5. Condition against using facts for commercial purposes. This is yet some other unreasonable circumstance on use of statistics obtained below RTI Act. The CBSE wanted the appellant to record an undertaking pronouncing he would no longer use it for business purposes. How can CBSE impose regulations

at the use of facts received with the aid of the citizen, which had been no longer imposed via the Right to Information Act, 2005.

CIC has handed following Directions/ Order:

1. The undertakings prescribed with the aid of the CBSE have the effect of significantly obstructing the get right of entry to information beyond what become permitted by the Right to Information Act, 2005. By prescribing such guidelines and implementing situations along with above, the CBSE tried to legislate something which is not prescribed or authorized by using the Parliament thru the Right to Information Act, 2005.

2. The Commission directs the CBSE to put in region such device with conducive practices by way of which the Right to facts of the appellants is not limited however facilitated, through eliminating the obstacles

inclusive of project to surrender their felony rights, as stated above.

3. The Commission in addition directs the CBSE to pay a compensation of Rs. 25,000/ to the appellant within 15 days from the date of receipt of this order for harassing him and compelling him to sign illegal challenge to surrender rights. The Commission directs the CBSE to provide the licensed copies of the answer scripts as required to the appellant, free of cost, inside 21 days from the date of receipt of this order.

- Massive stink over Planning Commission's Rs 35 lakh toilets:

The government may be speaking of austerity and curbing expenditure on diverse public schemes, but the Planning Commission must now not have were given that memo and an RTI application has discovered a big Rs 35 lakh to renovate two toilets at Yojana Bhavan.

According to the RTI application filed via activist Subhash Agrawal, not only had been the two bathrooms renovated for this sum, an extra 5 lakhs was spent on putting in a smart-card gadget which restricted access to the lavatories to 60 senior officers who work on the complex.

NDTV mentioned that the commission additionally planned to install protection cameras within the corridors main to these bathrooms to make sure device turned into not stolen. The 35-lakh lavatories have been, according to plans, to serve as fashions for upgrading another 3 bathrooms in the constructing at a later stage. Whether they would also have access through smart playing cards changed into no longer clear.

The petitioner S Agarwal meanwhile, hit out at the Planning Commission, and said his RTI application had revealed that another three such toilets were in the works. "It will not end here. Some other government and public offices will follow the same trend. This kind of wasteful expenditure when the government is talking about austerity and when the planning commissioner says that Rs 28 is the poverty line, is ridiculous", he said.

The revelations of the RTI utility has drawn big grievance from opposition parties. Senior BJP spokesman Balbir Punj stated that the revelation was 'shocking' and strongly condemned the move.

Meanwhile the information has precipitated the word Rs 35 Lakhs to start trending on Twitter, with some properly intentioned 'toilet humor'. @Roflindian said, "Spending Rs 35 lakhs for two toilets must be the most expensive way to relieve a south block in the morning", while @RameshSrivats said "By spending Rs. 35 lakhs on renovating two toilets. India has made it clear that it is an emerging superpower."

There have additionally been some obvious references made to the extravagance of the making plans commission, in particular evaluating the massive sum of money to the a great deal criticized Rs 28 urban poverty line that become determined upon by way of the members of the commission.

Travel expenses of Planning Commissioner Montek Singh Alhuwalia were also criticized in a recent report in The Hindu. Columnist P Sainath argued, based on RTI statistics received by different journalists, how big the foreign places journey charges of Montek, who is otherwise recognized for his justification of the poverty-line argument, had been. The highlight of Sainath's article changed into that the average every day fee of Alhuwalia become Rs. 2.02 lakhs during his foreign places tour among May and October closing year.

Using Montek's very own Rs 26 an afternoon calculation, this could have sustained a poor person in rural India for extra than 20 years!

Part – 2:

Funny RTI Stories in India

As Abraham Lincoln said "Government is of the people, by the people, for the people"

The authorities are our servant and we have no obligation to explain why we seek statistics from them. The government holds all the information in our behalf, in trust. Like a banker can't ask you why you need to peer your financial institution account statement, further the government can't deny if you ask them how they're governing our country. With the mechanism of RTI we can clearly participate within the operating of the authorities.

RTI or Right to Information is an act of Indian parliament that empowers the commonplace humans to seek statistics from the authorities. It empowers the Indian citizens to inspect the government work, take notes and get licensed photocopies to recognize the status of work.

It's been years since RTI Act came into existence to empower people and produce transparency to the system. However, people have been the use of it in instead unconventional ways. The queries that the government gets regularly fall in the range from being humorous to outright absurd.

In technical terms, those queries fall below the frivolous or vexatious category which means they denote a motion or the bringer of an action that is introduced without sufficient grounds for winning, merely to reason annoyance to the defendant. In the language of the internet, they have been filed simply to troll people.

Here are a number of the funniest RTI programs filed through people in India:

1. RTI for Indian nuclear release code:

A man has requested in his Right to Information query undoubtedly is too much of humorous. The Twitterati couldn't consider their eyes while Vivek Kumar, deputy secretary on the Prime Minister's Office (PMO) and an Indian Foreign Services (IFS) officer, shared on the micro blogging website that someone has filed a RTI seeking the release codes to India's nuclear arsenal. Could you agree with it?

Does the individual not recognize that nobody however the serving high minister of India has access to the launch codes of nuclear weapons? Please do now not take it as a joke, for statutory charge of Rs 10 had additionally been deposited in this regard. The application turned into manifestly rejected. It needed to be. It is a humorous tale of an RTI activist whose identity remained hidden.

2. RTI concerning Lord Venkateshwara:

Yes, you study that right. In 2014, Mr Narashimha Murthy, a social activist, allegedly filed a RTI to the TTD (Tirumala Tirupathi Devasthanam) trust wondering them whether or not Lord Venkateshwara's debt to Kubera had been cleared or how lots became nonetheless left. His basis of filing the RTI was his allegation that the agree with had hoodwinked the public by using weaving a tale approximately the Lord owing a debt.

A humorous RTI question has been made through a Bengalurean to Tirumala Tirupati Devastanam (TTD), inquiring for information about the cash Lord Venkateshwara has borrowed from Kubera on the time of his marriage with Padmavathi and what sort of he has returned. TTD is yet to present a reply. The RTI applicant alleges that TTD is hoodwinking humans through pointing out that the lord remains paying back interest for the principal amount he had borrowed from Kubera from the proceeds of the famous Tirupati 'Hundi'.

Narasimha Murty, a Bangalore-based RTI activist, visited Tirupati and saw a board which spoke about the money borrowed from Kubera, the lord of wealth, by

Lord Srinivasa and the need for the latter to pay hobby at the loan amongst different things. "After I saw the board, I become taken aback at the manner human beings are being fooled by way of this mythology. They all use god's call to make gains, which made me file this RTI query," Narasimha Murty stated.

Murty has addressed this RTI to the money owed officer and to the public information officer. "TTD says that the lord continues to be paying hobby to Kubera and it's far the cash given via devotees that best can help on this mission. As a citizen of this usa, I have all rights to recognize the bills of the TTD. But even after lots time, TTD has now not given me any information about the money owed. So, I have gone earlier than the Andhra Pradesh records commissioner. Even after repeating request letters, TTD isn't answering the questions I even have posed," Murty stated.

The story:

According to mythology, Lord Venkateshwara who become believed to be an incarnation of Vishnu, become named as Srinivasa. There turned into a king known as Akasha Raja who become ruling the nation that time. Many a time, Srinivasa quarrelled together with his divine consort Lakshmi and on one occasion came to Tirupati to do penance in an anthill. He became doing penance all day and nobody knew about this. Every day, one cow used to come back to that area and give milk to Srinivasa. Once the cow turned into back domestic, it stopped giving milk. Confused by using this, shepherds who had been looking after this cow followed it, and located it looking after Srinivasa who turned into inside the anthill. They went to hit the cow with a stick however to protect the animal, Srinivasa got here out and took the blows on his head.

While the attackers left the location, a bleeding Srinivasa was rescued by way of a woman referred to as Okkala Devi who took him to her vicinity and brought him up as her son. He commenced staying together with her and someday he saw Padmavathi, the Princes of the location. Srinivasa fell in love with her which she additionally reciprocated. Okkala Devi then approached the king Akasha Raja soliciting for him to permit the two to marry. The king requested Okkala Devi about her repute and about money she needed to behavior the wedding. It is at this juncture that Srinivasa changed into forced to visit Kubera, the lord of wealth and riches, for a loan. After processing the loan, Srinivasa were given to marry Padmavathi. Mythology says that from that day till date, Srinivasa is repaying Kubera his loan.

"Based on this story, the Devastanam nonetheless says that Lord Balaji is paying the hobby and it is pressuring devotees to provide more and more money. Emotional devotees believe all this and element with crores of rupees. I even have heard of wealthy people like the Amabanis, Vijay Mallya and several different politicians donating large sums to Lord Balaji. Is there an account for all this," Murty questions and says he will fight till he gets solutions for his questions?

Narasimha Murty is an RTI activist who has been fighting regarding the assets and the gold which came out after commencing of the doors at Padmanabha

Swamy temple in Kerala, in addition to the loss of life of an IAS officer who was searching after the temple. Post-this battle, Karnataka Golf Association was also declared a public authority based on his application.

Well, the tale within the News article has few discrepancies; nevertheless the gist is the identical. This must have probably been a creative petition to let the human beings suppose twice before donating on the temple.

3. RTI Query: "Whether Prime Minister Narendra Modi, earlier than he came into politics, worked in any Ramlila Troop? If yes, what position he played?"

The PMO responded: "Information sought isn't always a part of record."

4. RTI Query on of every other applicant desired to realize "how many and ⬚which sort of cylinder" had been "utilized in (the PM's) kitchen" in October 2014 and May 2015. The applicant also sought "copies of

payments of cylinders" and "copies of bills and spices" bought in May 2015.

The PMO replied: "The kitchen rate of the Prime Minister is personal in nature and no longer incurred on authorities account."

This alternate is simply one instance of the nature of queries referring to Prime Minister Narendra Modi which have been raised via applicants and replied to via the Prime Minister's Office (PMO) beneath the Right to Information (RTI) Act.

The under are some of the RTI Queries:

Q: Records and documents which display that the Prime Minister of India, Narendra Modi, is the Prime Servant of India and no longer the Prime Minister.

A: "There is not any concept to exchange the reputable designation of PM."

Q: Has the Prime Minister read the Indian constitution? Is the Prime Minister alleged to read the Indian constitution? Is the Prime Minister assumed to have examine Indian constitution? Has everybody inside the PMO till date advised the Prime Minister what his duties are closer to India?

A: "Information sought does not fall under the definition of records."

Q: Who allows the Prime Minister in sending tweets in nearby and overseas languages? Names of individual (s) for every regional language.

A: "Information sought is not maintained on record." (Another reply says that the "Prime Minister himself is dealing with his personal social media bills.")

Q: Number of ill or informal or fitness depart availed through the Prime Minister within the ultimate 10 years.

A: "No depart has been availed via the existing Prime Minister considering that taking up the workplace."

(Replying to a related question on whether Prime Minister Modi changed into on go away during the Bihar election campaign last year, the PMO responded: "Tours on election campaign aren't reliable.")

Q: Percentage of marks Modi secured at the same time as graduating in 1977 from Delhi University.

A: "Does not form part of records."

Q: Can one get the cell phone usages details of the PM underneath RTI?

A: "The PMO has now not given any cellular phone to Prime Minister."

Q: Legal repute of bulletins made by way of the Prime Minister.

A: "Once the assertion is made, the ministries worried are entrusted with the responsibility of implementing the announcements and tracking their implementation."

Q: Does the PMO communicate; send letters, etc., within the respectable language Hindi?

A: "Letters in Hindi obtained from Union Ministers, Governors, Chief Ministers, etc., are spoke back to in Hindi... Hindi letters from public are also replied in Hindi."

Q: Roza iftar parties Prime Minister Modi attended in 2014 and 2015.

A: "None."

And in the end this:

Q: Has the Principal Secretary to the PM, Nripendra Misra, ever taken his colleagues within the PMO on a picnic? If yes, who all went, how much money turned into spent, have been own family members additionally invited on such tour, and what turned into the meals menu? Was the meals ordered from an outside caterer? Was the venue constant by means of well-known consensus or changed into it decided entirely by way of Misra?

A: "No picnic/tour turned into ever organised through Nripendra Misra."

5. An RTI Application additionally requested Who officially declared Gandhi as Father of the Nation (given that we continually examine it in our textbooks)

The 10-year-old woman had filed an RTI query seeking facts on Gandhi Ji's title of 'father of nation'

In a written reply, the government stated that Mahatma Gandhi cannot be accorded the 'Father of the Nation' title by way of government as the Constitution does now not permit any titles except academic and navy ones.

While giving connection with the Article 18 (1) of the Constitution, the MHA had stated that it does now not allow any titles besides schooling and army ones.

The MHA had transferred her attraction to the National Archives of India.

The Central Information Commissioner Basant Seth then had stated, "There is not any order/file on record by which Gandhiji was given the identify of "Rastrapita".

Ans: No reliable declaration achieved until now.

6. Who declared Gandhi Jayanti, Republic day, Independence Day as countrywide holidays?

Ans: Such orders were by no means issued.

Bangalore, Aug 14: The reply to an RTI query has come as a surprise to all the ones Indians who believed that Aug 15, Jan 26 and Oct 2 are countrywide holidays.

Apparently, these three dates had been by no means notified with the aid of the government. It became the persistent efforts of one Aishwarya Parashar that revealed this extraordinary truth. Earlier this year in April, the 10-year-vintage had asked the Prime Minister's Office (PMO) for a duplicate of the unique Government Order (GO) that targeted the national holidays. The PMO surpassed on her question to the Ministry of Home, which in the beginning claimed that the matter does now not pertain to it. The Department of Personnel and Training (DoPT) ought to offer the answer, the Home Ministry averred. Finally, the latter clarified on May 17 that it couldn't find any Government Order (GO) that notified Republic Day, Independence Day and Gandhi Jayanti as countrywide holidays. Aishwarya was bemused through the respond due to the fact she has been taught in school that Jan 26, Aug 15 and Oct 2 are national holidays. When she filed an attraction to find out the truth, the appellate authority now not handiest showed that the Home Ministry's statement became accurate but also asked the National Archives to provide the 10-12 months-vintage a copy of the Government Order (GO) if any exists. A determined Aishwarya has considering the fact that shot off letters to the President and the Prime Minister, traumatic the Government Order (GO). Now the onus is on both Pranab Mukherjee and Manmohan Singh to meet her curiosity.

7. An RTI Applicate requested what's the Speed of internet on the PMO? Is his net faster than ours?

Brave Right to Information warriors have exposed how speedy Modi's Wi-Fi is! The average Indian gets 2Mbps, and Modi gets 34Mbps. (If you believe you studied that's fast, the 'Start-up Village' in Kochi has 1Gbps connectivity – 30 instances as fast as the PM's workplace!) The RTI additionally located that the PMO (Prime Minister's Office) uses Windows 7/Windows eight, and there's no money spent on jogging the @PMOIndia Twitter handle. While the RTI turned into brought in for transparency, a few geniuses are turning it right into a joke.

Sample these RTI petitions. Yes, these are real.

Ans: 34 Mbps.

8. Did that Hockey isn't always our National game?

This changed into discovered in an RTI filed by way of a category VII pupil, Aishwarya Parashar who sought data on a government order referring to India's countrywide game. Quite surprisingly, the Ministry of Youth Affairs and Sports in its response said that ministry has now not declared any game as its country wide game.

Same as ENERGY, STUPIDITY can be neither created nor be destroyed, however it transforms from one form to every other. All these does not end here handiest as many have requested:

• Can we've the election symbols with the rainbow filter? (On Voting Machines)

A political activist requested Election Commission of India why elections image used in electronic balloting machines are black and white and not colourful.

• An RTI doesn't absolutely have an age limit – legally, even a six-year antique can document one. And 9-year-old Pranav filed an RTI that forced the Delhi police to check in his stolen bike. He even requested for a Rs. 2500 compensation and demanded movement towards the assistant sub-inspector!

The police have been given a task by way of a 9-year-vintage boy named Pranav who used an RTI to pressure the police officers to record a FIR for his misplaced bicycle. The police had initially refused the to file the FIR for a trivial offense.

I have a feeling that this kid is going to develop up and do a few terrific stuffs.

• Do you realize what underpants should you wear before the Prime Minister?

It is one of the maximum absurd queries received by way of RTI act provoked by way of a ridiculous cause. A "troubled" citizen filed a petition asking what undergarments can be worn earlier than the Prime Minister. The question become asked without delay to the PMO's Office requesting the exact "specification of undergarments." Why? Because previously he had been arrested for stripping all the way down to his briefs scribbled with anti-government slogans in a central authority convention addressed by way of the PM.

I am so inspired via this man's guts.

• RTI vs. RTI!

In 2009, a Pune RTI activist found out how nearby politicians were the usage of the RTI to undercover agent on him and try to prevent him earlier than he revealed their unlawful activities!

• Um, simply for studies purposes.

An RTI applicant literally requested wherein exam papers for the Aligarh Muslim University were printed, and where they have been checked.

• Some humans can confuse RTI with Shaadi.Com

A man in his late forties from Kutch Gujarat filed a request under the RTI Act to provide data at the eligible females in the Government department for marriage. The request was made to the Tamil Nadu country statistics fee. In his application, he also stated the fact that an eligible bachelor from any government branch could do for him. He just genuinely desired to get married to a government employee.

- Kya Ache Din Aa Gaye Hain?

Someone literally asked the Prime Minister's workplace if "achhe din" are here. We can consider the reaction become "Work in progress"

- Time is money, however how a great deal cash exactly?

Time is cash, but how tons money is it consistent with Indian scriptures? An RTI requested the Punjab University this query.

- Saar, how much is cost of 1 wife @ MRP?

The same Punjab University RTI also asked how much a pretty and religious bride would cost, according to the Ramayana and the Mahabharata!

• How religious is the governor?

A resident of Hyderabad sought information from Andhra Pradesh governor on how typically he goes to temples in a day and also copy of the dinner menu hosted at his official residence.

• How much 'paan' do MCD officials clearly chew?

Blood pink stains might be compulsory artwork at every sarkari office, however this Delhi resident had had enough! He filed an application asking how tons 'paan' and tobacco an MCD legitimate consumes on common in a day, and even asked approximately the paan components!

• Where'd I gone wrong?

A wannabe Delhi University (DU) lecturer who didn't get the college job filed an RTI asking DU wherein his answers weren't as top as different individuals who applied.

• RTI = scholar discount?

A reproduction Delhi University marksheet fees Rs. 500. An RTI expenses Rs. 10. Which is why Delhi student's idea they'd get a reproduction marksheet for Rs. 10. Nah, it doesn't work like that.

• A disgruntled applicant wanted to realize if Arvind Kejriwal's reads the comments on his social media channels. In his application, he requested that when Arvind Kejriwal posts asks "silly and stupid questions" on Facebook and twitter, does he check the feedback he receives on such posts. This information being non-public in nature, can't be answered below RTI. Even then, it doesn't prevent people from trying their luck!

• A Delhi University scholar, filed an RTI against the girl he fell in love with. After few months of dating, he located out that she was married! He wanted to know what he can do to complain against her and get her punished for the mental discomfort she had caused.

• This is around the time our country directed numerous angers towards Fawad Khan. We had questions coming in asking if Fawad Khan turned into allowed to legally work and stay in India for his movie "Ae dil hai mushkil".

• An emotional applicant had requested whether astrologists and priests are authorized to declare a person a "manglik". If a person has "mangal dosh" and their partner dies, is there any purpose to trust that the "manglik" character is to be blamed? Quite a few RTI instances demand facts from spiritual bodies.

• Private organizations do no longer fall beneath RTI, that is a problem for many people. We obtained a question demanding call recording of a TataSky customer service name. Unfortunately, private companies are not required to answer RTI questions.

• RTI Registration quantity: MHOME/R/2016/50729:

Applicant   : Ajay Kumar

Information sought   : I am involved about the readiness of our government in the occasion of an invasion through Aliens Zombies and Extradimensional beings.

1. What are our probabilities towards them?

2. What way does the ministry of Home affair have at its disposal to defeat them?

3. Can we do it without Will Smith?

The authorities directly spoke back that statistics this is available may be shared under RTI. Since no info about hypothetical conditions is to be had, it can't be given. This must be the maximum well-mannered reply given below the RTI act!

• The applicant, a resident of Ahmedabad, had sought data approximately Mahatma Gandhi, a number of the former Presidents of India and other Ministers inquiring for their accurate date and time of birth, their blood institution and specifically their IQ.

• How many bullock cart tracks are in Delhi? How many trees inside the capital are inexperienced and what number of are dead? How many cups of tea are consumed up by the police personnel?

• Where did the laddoos go?

A UP lady despatched the erstwhile President George Bush some laddoos for 'Raksha bandhan'. Either he ate them and forgot approximately them, or his Secret Service did. Either way, she didn't get a thank you mail. Our brave female then approached the National Human Rights Commission to take action!

A UP girl requested NHRC on why 'ladoos' despatched with the aid of her to US President George W. Bush on 'Rakshabandhan'in no way reached him and requested the fee to take suitable motion.

• In January 2010, a 47-yr-antique man from Kutch, Gujarat, asked the Tamil Nadu state facts commission to provide him records on life partner for marriage from any govt department.

• How tons Maggie become wasted all through its ban?

• Please send sarkari wife!

A 47-year-antique guy requested the Tamil Nadu kingdom statistics commission to let him recognise about an appropriate life companion operating at any government branch.

• Who made you Bapu?

An elegance VI lady asked if MK Gandhi ever got an actual 'Father of the Nation' title. What became even more exceptional was that this become in 2012, while the Congress party was in power. The query went to the PMO, the Ministry of Home Affairs (MHA) after which to the National Archives of India– no one had an answer.

• Perhaps that is who human beings on Twitter seek advice from as 'chaddi warriors'!

An activist protested by way of stripping bare at a conference wherein former PM Manmohan Singh turned into speaking, and then filed an RTI asking the PMO if they needed to approve his logo of underwear!

• Someone requested about how a lot tea is utilized in Indian Army on each day bases.

• Haryana Police: Wives of Haryana Police officials filled a chain of RTIs, asking for the information related to the earnings in their husbands and what are their duty timings.

• RTI discovered how the President Pratibha Patil attempted to assemble a retirement domestic out of govt. funds a good deal in extra of her entitlement. It additionally revealed the masses of crores spent on her foreign travel which had little impact at the destiny of India.

• Hindi, now not a countrywide language: Court

Gujarat High Court has located that although majority of people in India have universal Hindi as a national language, there has been not anything on report to signify that any provision has been made or order issued affirming Hindi as a national language of India

The observation become made by using department bench of Chief Justice S.J. Mukhopadhaya and justice

A.S. Dave recently at the same time as rejecting a Public Interest Litigation (PIL) by way of one Suresh Kachhadia. Mr. Kachhadia had filed the PIL closing year searching for course to Central and State authorities to make it mandatory for manufacturers to print information of goods like price, elements, and date of manufacture in Hindi.

The court discovered, "Normally, in India, majority of the human beings have general Hindi as a country wide language and lots of human beings speak Hindi and write in Devanagari script but there's nothing on record to indicate that any provision has been made or order issued asserting Hindi as a country wide language of India." "No mandamus can be issued on any producer or others for giving details or details of package in Hindi in Devanagari script," it further stated.

It changed into contended by using Mr. Kachhadia's lawyer that Hindi become the country wide language and become understood by a large number of persons in India.

The Counsel representing central government submitted that unique provision has been made below the Standard of Weight and Measures (Packaged Commodities) Rules of 1977 that details of declaration have to be in Hindi in Devanagari script or in English.

The court stated that the Constituent Assembly while discussing the Language Formula observed the recommendation of the Sub-Committee on Fundamental Rights, which recommended the method as per which, "Hindustani, written either in Devanagari or the Persian script at the option of the citizen, shall, as the countrywide language, be the first reputable language of the Union. English shall be the second legitimate language for such period because the Union may, with the aid of law, determine."

However, inside the constitution, Hindi changed into declared as a reliable language and no longer a national language.

The court docket in its order stated Part XVII of the Constitution offers with Official Language. Under

Article 343, authentic language of the Union has been prescribed, which incorporates Hindi in Devanagari script and English.

• Highest wide variety of Indian prisoners are in Saudi Arabia:

As many as 6,569 Indian nationals are currently lodged in prisons of 67 overseas countries, inclusive of 254 in Pakistan shows an RTI question. The Arab countries crowned the list with Saudi Arabia (1691), Kuwait (1161) and UAE (1012), according to the records provided by way of the MEA on April 22 to attorney and RTI activist DB Binu. Italy has 121 Indian prisoners. The list also showed that UK has 426, USA 155, China 157, Bangladesh 62, Afghanistan 28, Bahrain 18 and Nepal 377 Indian prisoners.

• IIM exhibits admission standards:

Despite an excellent percentile Vaishnavi Kasturi, a visually-impaired pupil, in 2007 changed into denied a seat within the Indian Institute of Management in

Bangalore, one of the country's premier management institutes. She then filed an RTI application to request the institution to disclose the admission process.

Though Vaishnavi did now not get admission in any of the IIMs, her doubts over admission process were clarified. In a response to the question, the Chairman stated "CAT rankings are simply 1/5th of the standards for admissions. Forty in step with cent weight age is given for class X, XII and bachelor's ratings. Work revel in is given weight age too but it's mostly performance within the organization discussion and interview that counts which is as much as 35 per cent, plus 5 consistent with cent weight age is there when you have achieved a chartered accountancy course."

• The countrywide anthem of India does now not incorporate the phrase – "Sindh" – given that 1950.

Prof. Shrikant Malushte, a retired professor, challenged the phrase "Sindh" within the national anthem of India on the subsequent grounds:

"When Rabrindranath Tagore's poem become adapted by using the Constituent Assembly in 1950 as the national anthem, the phrase 'Sindh' was replaced with the aid of 'Sindhu' thinking about the fact that the region was a part of Pakistan partitioned from India. The newly replaced phrase Sindhu denotes the river that originated in Pakistan but flows thru the Indian valleys," stated 75-yr-antique Shreekanth Malushte.

However, despite the correction made with the aid of the Constituent Assembly, the government continued to prescribe the authentic poem written via Tagore, main to a scenario where the anthem turned into sung in two versions.

Prof. Shrikant then availed the RTI Act and received papers from the Ministry of Home Affairs which showed that the ideal version of the national anthem had the word 'Sindhu'. He then moved the Bombay High Court that agreed together with his observations and said that 'Sindh' in national anthem is probably a mistake and directed the center to offer its factor of view.

However, in 2005, the Supreme court docket had dismissed a comparable case by using mentioning that the real textual content contained "Sindh". Therefore, eventually the Bombay High court determined that 'Sindh will remain within the countrywide anthem'

• You recognize there's money being flushed down the toilet – or the Ganga, when start-ups can build empires from bedrooms, and but a single 'Clean Ganga' meeting charges over forty lakh Rupees. That became the budget for a single Vigyan Bhawan assembly through the Modi government's high-level group to easy the Ganga! This become revealed thru via RTI application.

They've one way or the other controlled to spend Rs 75,000 on "floral decorations"- and here's the alternative math:

Meetings and lodging of guests: Rs 26.7 lakh

Officials' journey: Rs 8.8 lakh

Advertising the occasion: Rs 5.1 lakh

Other arrangements: Rs 2.3 lakh

Actual Cleaning the Ganga: JEERO!

• If the legal age of a man to get sexually energetic is eighteen years and the legal age for him to get married is 21... Then what are we surely suggesting he need to do those three years?

• Now if the legal age for a man to get married is 21 years and the legal age for him to start drinking is 25 years... then how do you endorse he survives the first 4 years of marriage???

• The most awkward RTI demanded copies of all RTIs filed in India and their replies.

eBook disclaimer

Copyright notice:

Copyright © [2020] [Asha Kanta Sharma].

We control the copyright and other intellectual property rights in this eBook. Subject to the license below, all these intellectual property rights are reserved.

License to use eBook:

Subject to your [payment of the applicable price and] compliance with the restrictions below and the other terms of this disclaimer, we grant to you [a worldwide, non-exclusive and non-transferable license] to:

(a)   download a copy of the eBook;

(b)   store and view [a single copy] OR [up to [3] copies] of the eBook on desktop or notebook;

(c)   store and view [a single copy] OR [up to [3] copies] of eBook [reader] OR similar electronic [device]; and

(d)   print [a single copy] OR [up to [3] copies] of the eBook [solely [for your own personal, domestic and non-commercial use]].

You must not in any circumstances:

(a)   publish, republish, sell, license, sub-license, rent, transfer, broadcast, distribute or redistribute the eBook or any part of the eBook;

(b)   edit, modify, adapt or alter the eBook or any part of the eBook;

(c)   use the eBook or any part of the eBook in any way that is unlawful or in breach of any person's legal rights under any applicable law[, or in any way that is offensive, indecent, discriminatory or otherwise objectionable];

(d)   [use the eBook or any part of the eBook to compete with us, whether directly or indirectly]; or

(e)   [use the eBook or any part of the eBook for a commercial purpose].

You must retain, and must not delete, obscure or remove, all copyright notices and other proprietary notices in the eBook.

The rights granted to you by this disclaimer are personal to you, and you must not permit any third party to exercise these rights.

If you breach this disclaimer, then the license set out above will be automatically terminated upon such breach (whether or not we notify you of termination).

Upon the termination of the license, you will promptly and irrevocably delete from your computer systems and other electronic devices any copies of the eBook in your possession or control, and will permanently destroy any paper or other copies of the eBook in your possession or control.

Digital rights management:

You acknowledge that this eBook is protected by digital rights management technology, and that we may use this technology to enforce the terms of this disclaimer.

Pirate copies:

If you have bought or received a copy of this eBook from any source other than [Amazon.com], then that copy is a pirate copy. If this has happened to you, please let us know by email to [ashakantasharma@gmail.com].

You can buy a genuine copy of the eBook from [https://www.amazon.com/].

No advice:

The advice in this eBook is not substitute of any kind or form of legal advice. This is just a personal opinion of the author and based on life experiences which may not be perfect. The information is not advice and should not be treated as advice.

You must not rely on the information in the eBook as an alternative to [legal] OR [medical] OR [financial] OR [[any other matter]] advice from an appropriately qualified professional. If you have any specific questions about any such matter you should consult an appropriately qualified professional.

If you think you may be suffering from any medical condition you should seek immediate medical attention. You should never delay seeking medical advice, disregard medical advice, or discontinue medical treatment because of information in the eBook.

You should never delay seeking legal advice, disregard legal advice, or commence or discontinue any legal action because of information in the eBook.

Limited warranties:

Whilst we endeavor to ensure that the information in the eBook is correct, we do not warrant or represent its completeness or accuracy.

We do not warrant or represent that the use of the eBook will lead to any particular outcome or result.[In particular, we do not warrant or represent that by using the eBook you will [specify non-warranted outcome].]

To the maximum extent permitted by applicable law, we exclude all representations, warranties and conditions relating to this eBook and the use of this eBook.

Limitations and exclusions of liability:

Nothing in this disclaimer will:

(a)   limit or exclude any liability for death or personal injury resulting from negligence;

(b)   limit or exclude any liability for fraud or fraudulent misrepresentation;

(c)   limit any liabilities in any way that is not permitted under applicable law;

(d)   exclude any liabilities that may not be excluded under applicable law; or

(e)   limit or exclude any mandatory rights that you have as a consumer under applicable law.

The limitations and exclusions of liability set out in this disclaimer:

(a)   are subject to the preceding provision; and

(b)   govern all liabilities arising under this disclaimer or relating to the subject matter of this disclaimer, including liabilities arising in contract, in tort (including negligence) and for breach of statutory duty, except to the extent expressly provided otherwise in this disclaimer.

We will not be liable to you in respect of any losses arising out of any event or events beyond our reasonable control.

We will not be liable to you in respect of any business losses, including (without limitation) loss of or damage to profits, income, revenue, use, production, anticipated savings, business, contracts, commercial opportunities or goodwill.

We will not be liable to you in respect of any loss or corruption of any data, database or application.

We will not be liable to you in respect of any special, indirect or consequential loss or damage.

Trade marks:

Our logos and our other registered and unregistered trade marks are trade marks belonging to us; we give no permission for the use of these trade marks, and such use may constitute an infringement of our rights.

The third party registered and unregistered trade marks and service marks that feature in our eBook are the property of their respective owners and, unless stated otherwise in this disclaimer, we do not endorse and are not affiliated with any of the holders of any such rights and as such we cannot grant any license to exercise such rights.

Law and jurisdiction:

This disclaimer shall be governed by and construed in accordance with [Indian law] and any disputes relating to this disclaimer shall be subject to the Guwahati, Assam jurisdiction of the courts of [India].